PREFAC

Over the years, the walks in this book have b
The children began them at about the age of
greater degree of difficulty, fourteen years l
We have read various guide books whilst
However, we have not found many suitab..._ ... ._ ,
scrambles. With this book, therefore, we have attempted to introduce a series of walks
which involve various degrees of effort, but will also provide great enjoyment by all
the family.

Families who wish to sample the delights and splendours of these incomparably
beautiful fells and dales, will, hopefully, not be disappointed.

Parents, ensure that this book is retained for posterity and your old age. The time
will come when family walks are all that you are able to manage. If you take time,
care and patience with your children, you will be rewarded in later life when they ask
you to join them on these walks. (You may even find that they might be prepared to
carry your rucksack)!

Timothy and Sylvia Bunker
January 1996

ABOUT THE AUTHORS

Sylvia was born in the Peak District of Derbyshire, whilst Timothy originated from
Warwickshire. They met at their climbing club and, after marriage, have lived for the
past eighteen years in Cumbria; where they have raised their family and enjoyed
frequent expeditions, with their children, in the northern fells.

Timothy is a quantity surveyor and arbitrator in the construction industry, whilst
Sylvia is involved in teaching support within the local junior school.

DEDICATION

To our sons Martin and Christopher
&
Grandma Lillian

Herdwick Ram

Family Walks around Keswick and Northern Lakeland

Timothy and Sylvia Bunker

HIGH INTEREST · LOW MILEAGE

Scarthin Books of Cromford
Derbyshire
1996

Family Walks Series

THE COUNTRY CODE

Guard against all risk of fire
Fasten all gates
Keep dogs under proper control
Keep to paths across farmland
Avoid damaging fences, hedges and walls
Leave no litter
Safeguard water supplies
Protect wildlife, plants and trees
Go carefully on country roads
Respect the life of the countryside

Published by Scarthin Books, Cromford, Derbyshire, 1996

Phototypesetting by Paragon Typesetters, Newton-le-Willows, Merseyside

Printed by Redwood Books

Maps by Ivan Sendall

Photographs by Timothy and Sylvia Bunker

Cover photograph: Timothy and Sylvia Bunker

ISBN 0 907758 93 2

Contents

Map of the Area

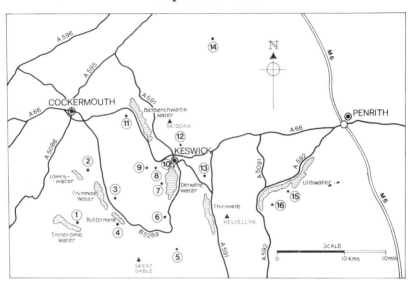

The duck pond at Caldbeck (Route 14)

Introduction

It is no pleasure to be out on the fells, or to be walking the valleys, with a child or children who are either bored or overstretched. Plan your route carefully, with these thoughts in mind.

Care must be taken, as all these journeys are through a mountain landscape and children must be looked after to avoid hazards.

The children are the next generation of walkers and must be carefully encouraged to enjoy and respect the more rugged parts of the country and the people who live there. We have tried to introduce some entertaining interest, or novelty, into each of the walks. Parents will find reward in beautiful, far reaching vistas; but, the younger members of the party are frequently enthralled by the details at their feet, or a story about the route.

The Lake District's beauty was initially brought to the public's attention through the classic writings of the "Lakes Poets", but Beatrix Potter's "Peter Rabbit" and Arthur Ransome's "Swallows and Amazons" showed that this is also the landscape for children's adventures.

Walks for children need to progressively unfold like the pages of a story book. They will find little enjoyment in labouring through peat bog and bracken, across trackless fellside, towards a distant and noble objective.

Choosing a walk

Choose a walk which is comfortably within the capabilities of ALL of the family. If the family is not used to walking on the fells, it is sensible to start on low level valley and lakeside walks; and perhaps progressing to higher altitudes as experience develops.

Paths

Walks in this book are chosen to follow well defined tracks for most of their length. Please bear in mind that children are much more comfortable whilst following an established path, than taking rougher cross country routes. Do not seek to take short cuts, thus minimising erosion and avoiding crags or other difficulties.

Maps

We have tried to present clear and helpful maps with each of these routes; but they can be no substitute for the unsurpassed Ordnance Survey maps. Obtain the relevant O.S. map for your walk.

The area covered by this book is included within Ordnance Survey 1:25000 scale maps:- "The English Lakes" — "North West Sheet" and "North East Sheet" (with the exception of the Caldbeck route — which is O.S. "path finder" sheet 567/576).

Their purchase is repaid many times over by the peace of mind they impart and, next to a "Family Walks" book, they are the best holiday souvenir you can have.

Use the sketch maps to choose and identify your route, then follow it on the Ordnance Survey map, before actually starting the walk, and do not forget to pack it in your rucksack before setting off.

Refreshments

In common with other volumes within the "Family Walks" series, we have included cafes and pubs where children are welcome. However, ALWAYS carry drinks for all of the family, together with nourishing and high energy food on the fells, such as honey sandwiches and chocolate bars.

Do not rely upon descending to eat in a cafe in the valley. Stopping for a picnic on the walk is a source of considerable pleasure to children, but make sure that parents carry the food! The rucksack in our family has become known as the slow food restaurant which the children must accompany closely, because opening times are sudden and unpredictable.

Equipment (for the valleys)

Whilst rambling along valley and lakeside routes, it is obviously sensible to carry, or wear, warm, windproof and waterproof clothing (just as you would expect for a country ramble within other areas of the country). Trainers may be sufficient if it is dry underfoot, but Wellington boots will often be more suitable.

Equipment for the high ground.

As the children's interest and capabilities develop and you choose a fell walk, the following equipment is *ESSENTIAL* to your family's safety and comfort.

1. Boots with vibram soles or equivalent. (many climber's shops operate rental schemes)

2. Good quality cagoules and overtrousers that are both waterproof and windproof. Buy slightly large to be grown into. (It doesn't matter-they won't be fashion items and can be passed down through the family).

3. Suitable and warm clothing that may be worn under waterproofs. Fleece jackets are currently reccommended, along with a brand of trousers known as "Ron Hill Tracksters" or "Karrimor Kragsters". These are inexpensive and available for children. Polyester-cotton trousers are also reccommended as quick drying clothing.

4. Warm hat and gloves.

5. A compass and appropriate O.S. map (make sure that you can use them)

6. An emergency plastic survival bag.

7. Suitable rucksacks to carry the family's clothing and refreshments. Try to share the load between the family, but be cautious with who carries the chocolate biscuits. Do not turn Father into an overburdened packhorse!

8. IMPORTANT! WHEN WALKING IN THE MOUNTAINS, ALWAYS ENSURE THAT EMERGENCY PROVISIONS ARE CARRIED AT ALL TIMES. (SUCH AS KENDAL MINT CAKE, GLUCOSE TABLETS OR CHOCOLATE).

9. Torch and whistle in case of emergency. Six repeated short blasts on the whistle. (Do not allow children to play with the whistle, the Mountain Rescue are not amused)!

We hope that the above list does not appear to be too daunting, but please follow this advice and let the mountain rescue lads sleep at night.

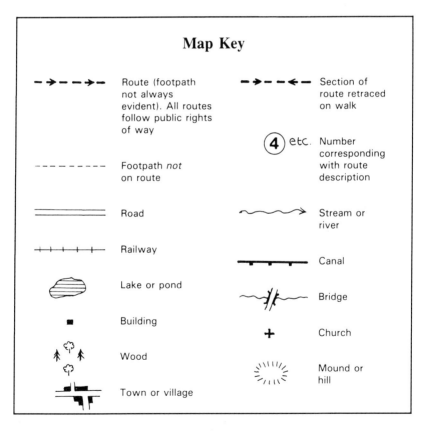

Map Key

➤ ➤ ➤	Route (footpath not always evident). All routes follow public rights of way
- - - - - - - -	Footpath *not* on route
═══════════	Road
+—+—+—+—+—	Railway
Lake or pond	
■	Building
Wood	
Town or village	
➤ ➤ ◄	Section of route retraced on walk
④ etc.	Number corresponding with route description
∿➤	Stream or river
▬▬▬▬	Canal
∿≠≠∿	Bridge
✚	Church
⌇⌇⌇	Mound or hill

Evening over Ennerdale

Around Ennerdale Water

Grading: moderate (100 yards scramble). NOT suitable for Toddlers

Outline

Bowness Knot car park — River Lisa bridge — around Ennerdale Water — Bowness Knot car park.

Summary

A journey around Ennerdale Water across open meadows, through ancient woodland and across rough craggy fellside.

Attractions

An interesting and varied path completing the circuit of the lake, set against the backcloth of Lakeland peaks in one of the quieter corners of the Lake District.

This is a generally quiet, secluded and wild valley, heavy glaciation, skyline notched by distinctive and famous peaks, such as Steeple and Pillar. There is much coniferous forest further up the valley, but this walk takes you into some of the indigenous oak woodland.

You will see numerous directions for alternative forestry commission routes further up the valley which make for excellent alternative days out.

Interesting boulders to clamber on around the lake on the Anglers' Crag bank. Very young children might find the route awkward.

(General note: Obviously, since this route circumnavigates the lake, no short cuts are available.)

Best and driest picnic spots

Just before you reach Anglers' Crag. By the car-park and various unofficial sites around the lake shore.

Refreshments

At the Fox and Hounds in Ennerdale Bridge. (High-chair provided).

11

Route 1

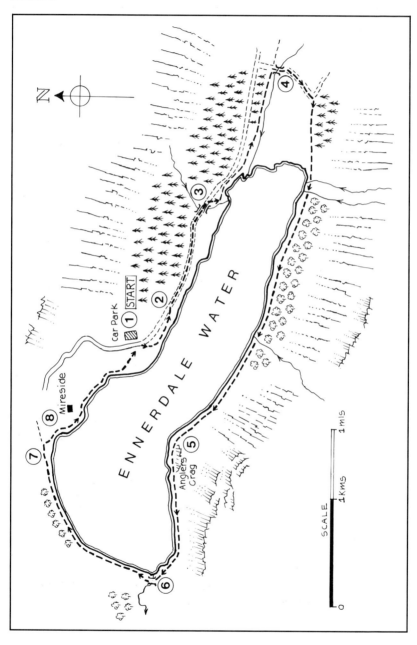

Route 1

Around Ennerdale Water 7 miles

Start

Bowness Knot car park (O.S. grid reference: NY 109154). Approached by minor roads off the A5086 Cockermouth-Egremont road.

Route

1. *Walk out of the car park exit, past the forestry commission sign across the road and down the hill through the bracken to the lake shore, where you meet the shoreside path. Turn left and follow the path along the lake shore.*

2. *After about half a mile, meet the forest track and continue along it beside the lakeshore. (Beware with the children. This track sees little traffic, but you may possibly meet some cars or logging trucks along the way).*

3. *After approximately another half mile, the lakeside path recommences. Take this more attractive route, subsequently meeting the river Lisa and it's confluence with Ennerdale Water. Follow the river side path upstream.*

   Cross the river at the forestry road bridge. Ignore the various entrances into fields and continue across the valley along the forest track.

4. *Immediately before the gated entrance to forestry on the forest side of the valley, climb the wooden ladder stile to your right and follow the path back towards the lake skirting the perimeter of the woodland. Meet up again with the lake shore, entering the indigenous oak woodland. The path becomes interesting as it passes over footbridges and stiles through the woodland.*

5. *The bouldery scramble round the point of Anglers' Crag, is very easy and great fun, but don't let your children wander off the track. After a short scramble around the crag the scenery widens out.*

6. *Towards the end of the lake, leaving the rocky landscape behind, the path bends to the right through a kissing gate set in a stone wall. Go across a footbridge over a little beck and down a fenced path to cross the substantial footbridge over the outlet from the lake. Pass through the kissing gate opposite and continue across the meadow parallel with the lake shore. (Ignore the gate on your right). Continue following the fence line around the shore, through another kissing gate and then to more woodland along the lake shore.*

   (Green Gable can be glimpsed through the notch in the skyline between Pillar rock and Bowness knot which is an outlier to Herdus).

13

7. *At the junction with a tractor track, turn right and continue to follow the Lake shore past the National Trust sign. After passing through another kissing gate, the path curves slightly uphill through the gorse bushes away from the lake shore.*

8. *Immediately after a timber stile turn right down a stone track back towards the shore. Cross a timber footbridge over the beck past the final stile. As you approach Bowness Knot, the path climbs away up the fellside and meets a lane running between stone walls. Turn right and follow this green lane, with the rocky knoll on your right, and emerge back at the car park.*

Mellbreak

14

Mellbreak

Height: 1,676 feet (511 metres). Grading: Very strenuous!

Outline

Loweswater − Mellbreak (North Summit) − Mellbreak (South Summit) −
Mosedale − Loweswater

Summary

The direct route is a short, but very rugged excursion, which is not recommended for parties which have little experience of the mountains. This route is a must for those parties who have found that all other walks within this book are a lazy doddle and require a short and sharp introduction into the more extensive challenges, achievements and enjoyment that the mountains offer.

An easier alternative is also included.

Attractions

Beautiful views across Crummock Water, Loweswater Lake and the Vale of Lorton.

The walk is off the more intensely beaten track, up a superbly rugged little mountain which is not overshadowed by any close neighbours.

Refreshments

The "Kirkstile Inn" in Loweswater.

Route 2

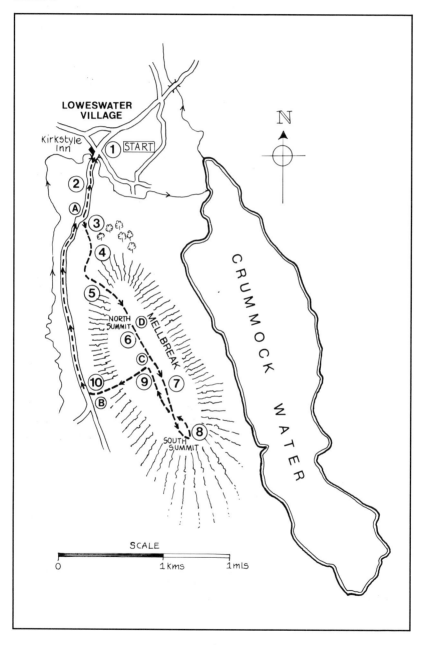

Route 2

Mellbreak   5½ miles

Start

This walk starts from the Kirkstile Inn in Loweswater, (O.S. Grid reference 141209) which is approached along approximately two miles of minor roads, off the B5289, Lorton to Buttermere road.

Route

1. *Start the walk by passing to the left of the Kirkstile Inn, down the narrow tarmac lane, and within a few yards, turn right at an old signpost which helpfully directs "No road to the lake" in two directions. Follow the lane behind the Inn, over Church Bridge, up the hill to pass Kirkhead farm; (it continues as a stone tractor track.)*

2. *Follow the stone walled track between the fields towards the woodland beyond. Ignore any field gateways to either side.*

3. *After approximately half a mile of walking from the inn, the tractor track passes through a gateway, then contours right below a steep forested part of the fell. This is where you will continue directly up the steep hill along the forest fire break.*

4. *Leave the firebreak and walk across the open fellside along a grassy winding path towards a patch of light coloured scree on the flank of the mountain.*
   The enthusiasm of some of the party may begin to wane as this scree slope is approached. Take advantage of the track slanting up to your left which becomes a zigzagging route separating the mass of scree from the heather. Climb up the face of the mountain, avoiding the more unstable sections. Any attempts at a "bee-line" will be regretted. Climb carefully on a short, but rather looser section between some small rock outcrops, taking advantage of each and every zig and zag that is offered.

5. *Follow the track, on terra firma, through the heather slanting up to left; and clamber up the broad rocky ridges onto easier ground beyond, continuing to the grassy north summit of the mountain. The gentle grassy top is reached within 1½ miles. A short but intense journey that will not readily be forgotten.*

6. *From the top, turn in a southerly direction to descend a few hundred feet to the saddle. Do not try to go down the way you came up! There is a clear path down to the saddle. After 1½ miles a path veers off to the right. This is the way down if you do not wish to attempt the south summit.*

7. *Follow the grassy path along broad ridge ahead of you up to the South Summit. (There is a wonderful view looking down to Buttermere and Crummock water.) Three quarters of a mile separates the two peaks.*

8. *Retrace your steps back to the col between the summits.*

9. *Turn left (West) when you regain the col and follow the steep path down into Mosedale.*
   Do not be diverted off onto any of the many sheep tracks.

10. *When you reach the valley floor, turn right along a broad green track and stride out for home. The track becomes wider and stony and passes, to the lower edge of woodland, to rejoin the route of ascent at the foot of forest ride. (At point 3 of ascent).*

Alternative easier route

a. *At point 3 of main route, turn right on stone track alongside wall. Follow this track up the valley for approximately 1½ miles.*

b. *Turn left up the steep track to reach the ridge, at the col, between the two peaks.*

c. *On top of the broad ridge, turn left to north summit.*

d. *Reverse this route for the descent (points 8 to 10 of main route).*

Crummock Water from Rannerdale Knotts

Rannerdale Knotts

Height 1,160 feet (354 metres)
Grading: Moderate (initial strenuous steep section)

Outline
Buttermere Hause car park − Rannerdale Knotts summit − Rannerdale valley −
Buttermere Hause car park

Summary
A rugged "mini peak", with a descent down a secluded valley.
There is the alternative of a gentle ascent which can return by the same route

Attractions
Rannerdale Knotts is an impressively rugged little peak, standing clear of the mass
of the higher fells, to protrude out into the valley holding Crummock Water and Lake
Buttermere. The obvious attractions of this route include the opportunity to linger at
height whilst you gradually descend along the long grassy ridge, giving beautiful
views down to Crummock Water, the village and the lake of Buttermere It is backed
by the High Stile ridge with Great Gable in the distance.

A less obvious attraction is the section of the walk down the peaceful and secluded
valley of Rannerdale.

An unusual feature of this route is that the old Buttermere Hause (at the head of
Rannerdale) is an ancient battle site between the Norman invaders and the locals. The
locals won!

Refreshments
There are two inns within the village of Buttermere, which both serve meals.

19

Route 3

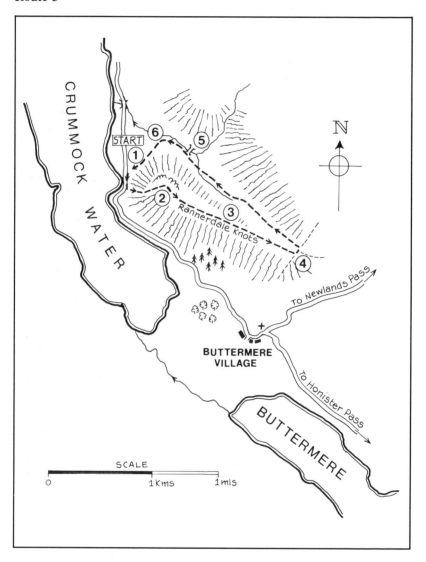

Route 3

Rannerdale Knotts   3 miles

Start

Car park situated at Buttermere Hause (O.S. Grid Reference NY 163184), and approached by the B5289 Cockermouth to Buttermere road.

Route

1. *After leaving the car park, turn left along the tarmac road for approximately 75 yards, before slanting left up a path rising between the bracken towards a shoulder on the mountain.*

2. *Ignore the path which branches left before you reach this shoulder. Upon reaching the shoulder, the path turns to the left and rises steeply towards the main ridge of the mountain. A brief steep section of scree is unavoidable along a short section of this part of the route. After the scree, and a false summit, the path wends up a wide grassy rake between rock buttresses to join the main ridge. Follow the broad, grassy and generally trackless ridge to your right, up to the main summit.*

3. *Continue, in a generally south easterly direction, along the top of the knobbly ridge past the second, and slightly lower, summit. Follow the path down the short rocky outcrop, and reach the gentle grassy promenade to stroll out down the mile long undulating ridge. Do not be tempted to try to contour round any of the bumps on this ridge, or to branch off down to the valleys on either side.*

4. *At the end of this ridge you meet a "Five Ways" junction of grassy pathways through the bracken. Turn acutely left (North-West) on a "hairpin" to drop into Rannerdale Valley, walking parallel to the main ridge that you have just descended. This easy and pleasant path follows a steady descent down the length of the valley.*

5. *Ignore the footbridge to your right. Towards the lower portion of this valley, the path runs beside a stone wall. Turn right through the gate in this wall, but do not cross the footbridge across the beck below you.*

6. *Follow the fainter path, on the left hand bank of this beck, to descend below the crags of Rannerdale Knott. Follow the foundations of an old stone wall. Ahead of you, Rannerdale Farm comes into view, but continue to curve to the left, beside a high stone wall. Pass through a kissing gate, below Dale How to rejoin the car park.*

Alternative route:

If the party would prefer not to take the steep ascent from Buttermere Hause car park, there is an alternative route from Buttermere village. Leaving the B5289 road at Hagg Sike (O.S. Grid Reference 173174) to rise up the gently climbing path towards Whiteless Pike. Upon reaching the five way junction of paths, turn left (North-West) up the broad ridge of Rannerdale Knotts to the summit. Return by reversing this route.

21

The tunnel by Buttermere

Around Buttermere

Grading: Easy

Outline

Fish Hotel car park — Buttermere Lake — Gatesgarth Farm — Wilkinsyke farm — Fish Hotel car park.

Summary

This walk is carried out anti-clock wise around the lake. A suitable wet weather walk when the fell tops are out of bounds.

Attractions

A very pleasant and undulating path through mixed woodland interspersed with open meadows around a beautiful lake. There is the novelty of a tunnel carved out of the rock. Fields at the South East end of the lake are the venue for "One Man and His Dog". There is plenty of woodland that children can safely play in, and a spectacular waterfall in the hills (Sour Milk Gill)

Refreshments

The Fish Hotel, Croft House Cafe and the Bridge Hotel — All in Buttermere village.

Route 4

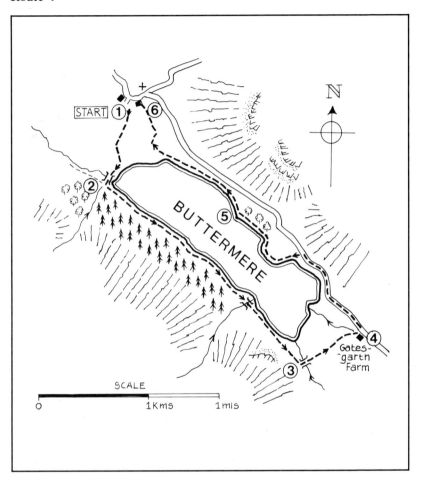

Route 4

Around Buttermere   4¾ miles

Start

Car park situated between Fish Hotel and Bridge Hotel (O.S. Grid reference: NY 175170), Approached by the B5289 road between Cockermouth and Keswick.

Route

1. *From the Fish Hotel take the Bridleway sign posted to Buttermere Lake. Follow this stony track, ignoring the turning to Scaleforce, on the right, or any other turnings to left or right.*

2. *Head across the valley floor towards Sour Milk Gill waterfall. Turn right when the lake comes into view after the third kissing gate, cross the footbridge, and enter the woodland. Turn left before the foot of Sour Milk Gill waterfall, following the path with the lake shore on your left. Ignore any paths off.*

3. *Cross the footbridge, go through a kissing gate in a stone wall and leave the woodland.Ignore the track rising to Scarth Gap on your right. On reaching a circular stone sheep fold, turn left through a kissing gate and cross the footbridge towards Gatesgarth Farm.*

4. *At the farm, turn left along the Buttermere road (beware of the traffic). The road regains the lake shore. After 100 yards, take the path on the left, which closely follows the lake shore, then go through a kissing gate, across open meadow and round woodland.*

5. *Pass through two kissing gates and eventually enter the tunnel. The path continues along the lake shore through various kissing gates, across a stone footbridge and up a rocky headland, following the path back to the farm.*

6. *Cross the stile into the farm yard and back to the car park in the village.*

Crossing Stockly Bridge

Route 5   **8 miles**
**(may be shortened to 6 mile or 6½ mile if optional extra
routes are not included)**

Styhead Tarn & Sprinkling Tarn

Grading: strenuous

Outline
Seathwaite— Stockley Bridge — Styhead Tarn — Sprinkling Tarn —
Ruddy Gill — Grains Gill — Stockly Bridge — Seathwaite

Summary
A walk in between the high fells, mainly along ruggedly constructed stone footpaths.

Attractions
The interests of this walk lie both within the past as well as in the present. Neolithic man used these routes to transport his roughly hewn stone axes from their "factories" on the steep fellsides of the Langdale Pikes, Glaramara and Scafell Pikes to the finishing and polishing sites on the West Cumberland coast. It was these axes which enabled the deforestation of the heavily wooded fells to create the upland pastures that we see today. In later years, strings of packhorses were the long distance lorries of the 18th and 19th centuries, as they threaded their way along these skilfully constructed tracks to link the villages, market towns and the coastal ports. More recently, these ancient routes suffered disastrously from the erosion of thousands af walking boots, but an enormous amount of very hard work has repaired many of these tracks and contributed towards healing the open scars of erosion across the fells. So, use these stone paved zig-zags, do not cut the corners, and allow the mountain sides to recover their greenery. . The attraction is that, by linking a number of these old routes, a journey can be made into the heart of impressive and beautiful mountain country, without the commitment of taking a family onto the highest ridges and summits.

Refreshments
The tea shop at Seathwaite Farm.

Route 5

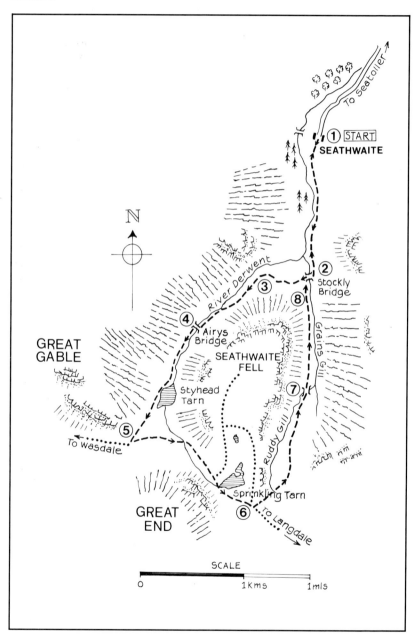

Route 5

Styhead Tarn & Sprinkling Tarn   8 miles
(may be shortened to 6 mile or 6½ mile if optional extra routes are not included)

Start

Commence this walk at Seathwaite (O.S. Grid reference : 235122), approached off the B5289 from Seatoller.

Route

1. *Walk South, through the farmyard, ignoring any turns to either side, to follow the broad stony path, through the field gate, and along the flat valley floor.*

2. *After two stiles, alongside field gates, the path reaches Stockly Bridge. Turn right, and cross the stone packhorse bridge, pass through the wooden gate facing you, · and climb steeply up the stone paved zig zags on the open fellside.*

3. *The path goes through a wooden gate in a stone wall, (This is the top of this set of steep zig zags and a Mars Bar may provide the children with some much needed battery charging before continuing the journey) and then follows the South-Eastern bank of the infant River Derwent.*

4. *Cross the river by a timber footbridge, and continue upstream along the other bank.*

5. *Walk past Styhead Tarn and continue in a South-Westerly direction, up to the mountain rescue stretcher box, just below the summit of Styhead Pass. Turn left at the stretcher box (East) to follow the track which runs along the watershed between Borrowdale and Wasdale, then climbs around the foot of the crags of Great End.*

Shorter Optional Route

A short, but rewarding detour can be made to continue, beyond the stretcher box, in a South-Westerly direction to the summit of the pass, to peek round the flanks of Great Gable down into Wasdale. Then, return to the stretcher box. Extra half a mile.

Longer Optional Route overleaf

Longer Optional Route

On reaching Sprinkling Tarn, turn left (North) over open fellside, climbing between small crags and tarns, to reach the summit of Seathwaite Fell. This extra route is generally pathless, but supplies a beautiful and little visited mini-peak spectacularly situated amongst the famous giants. The views are superb. Then retrace your footsteps back to Sprinkling Tarn. This is a wonderful landscape for exploring. This adds an extra 1½ mile to your journey

6. *After passing Sprinkling Tarn, the path initially rises, then descends to the head of the ravine of Ruddy Gill. Turn left to cross the gill at the stepping stones and follow the made track, descending in a Northerly direction, above the steep eastern bank of the ravine.*

7. *Cross the timber footbridge over Ruddy Gill, and continue downhill along the path on the western bank of Grains Gill.*

8. *Pass through a wooden gate in a stone wall and rejoin your route of ascent at Stockly Bridge (point 2. above). Cross the bridge and retrace your steps to Seathwaite.*

Climbing through Johnny's Wood

30

Johnny's Wood — Seatoller

Grading: Easy (30 yards moderate scramble alongside the river)

Outline

Seatoller Car Park — Johnny's Wood — Seatoller Car Park.

Summary

A gentle woodland and riverside walk.

Attractions

The opportunity to walk through secluded woodland which provides peace and tranquillity away from the every day crowds! Having entered through the "Jaws of Borrowdale", you are surrounded by mountains which tower above, yet you remain hidden in ancient oak woodland. The path meanders, in a delightful fashion, up hill and down dale and passes beside babbling brooks and rivers, before returning once more to the car park. This woodland walk is greatly recommended for younger children.

After heavy rain, it is wise to equip your family in wellington boots for this walk.

Best picnic spot:

Sitting on the bench outside the Youth Hostel overlooking the river.

Route 6

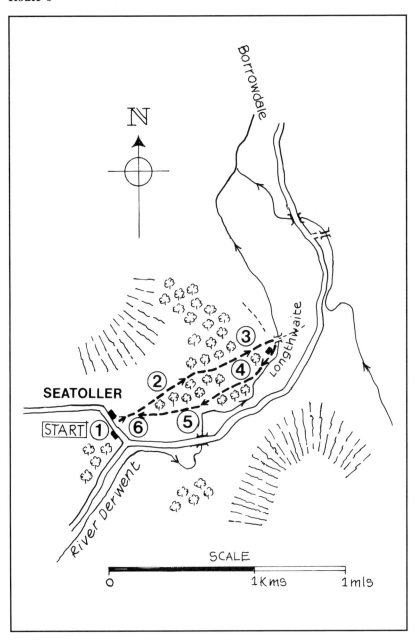

Route 6

Johnny's Wood − Seatoller   2 miles

Start

Start this walk from the car park at Seatoller. (also the terminus for the "Borrowdale Bus"). (O.S. grid reference: 244137)

Route

1. *Follow the path up the fellside, from the car park to a timber stile in the stone wall.*

   Turn right along a wide, and initially stony, path slanting up the fell away from this wall. After approximately 100 yards, ignore the farm track which veers up the fell to your left.

2. *On reaching a crossroads of paths, turn right and pass through a gate in a wire fence into the woodland.*

   Continue along a broad track, through woodland, ignoring all turnings off to left or right.

   On meeting a tall, substantial stone wall, pass through the gap.

3. *Walk down the steep hillside − careful in wet weather − (slightly awkward rocky section, take care of young children) − to reach the field.*

   Cross the field and climb a wooden stile in the wire fence,and turn right following the path alongside the fence.

4. *Continue past Longthwaite Farm, through the kissing gate, and onto Longthwaite Youth Hostel. The path passes in front of the hostel. Follow the track through the kissing gate in the wooden fence, and along the river side.- Awkward rocky section. Follow the path around the rocky headland and through another kissing gate.*

5. *Pass through a farm gate and climb up the path to your right.*

   Follow the path behind the large Christian Fellowship hostel, and through a kissing gate in a stone wall.

6. *Turn left alongside the wall and return to the car park.*

Awaiting a "short cut" home

Around Derwentwater
(including sections travelled by Ferry service)

Grading: Easy

Outline
Ferry from Keswick landing stage to Lodore — High Brandlehowe —
Low Brandlehow — Hawse End — Nichol End — Portinscale — Keswick —
Keswick Landing Stage.

Summary
A lakeside walk through meadowland and broadleafed woodland.

Attractions
This is an unusual excursion, in that walkers may use the circular ferry service to vary
the route to the shorter alternatives described in the text. There are beautiful views
across the lake towards Skiddaw and up the valley into the "Jaws of Borrowdale".
The walk is also novel by using long sections of "duckboards", raised above the
marshland which children will enjoy. The route provides a contrast with the sylvan
beauty of the woodland alongside the lake compared to the bustle of the town centre.

Refreshments
Lakeside tea gardens next to Keswick landing stage and numerous cafes and pubs in
Keswick.

Route 7

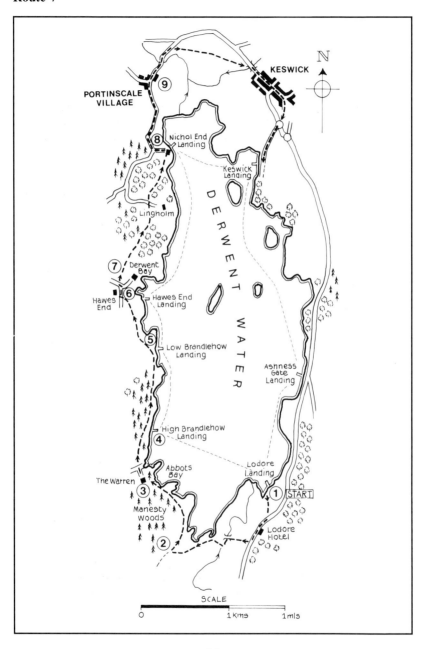

Route 7

Around Derwentwater

6¾ miles
(with 4 shorter alternatives)

Start

From the Derwentwater landing stage at Keswick, (O.S. Grid Reference NY 264228) collect your boat ticket for the clockwise service around the lake (having first ascertained boat times), and travel on the ferry to the landing stage at Lodore. Alight here.

Route

1. *From the Lodore landing stage, walk along the track towards the road. At the road, turn right and after ¾ mile turn right to the sign post to Manesty. Cross the river Derwent by "Chinaman's Bridge". Follow along the "duck board" path through the rushes, until you join the main path along the lake shore.*

2. *Continue along further "duck boards" (take care of young children, the marsh is very wet!) The main path eventually veers away from the lake shore to pass through a timber gate in a stone wall through Manesty Woods.*

3. *At "The Warren", turn right along a tarmac drive to Abbotts bay, then turn left on a track towards Brandlehowe cottage. After passing the cottage turn right through a gate in the fence into woodland, meandering past old mining spoil heaps.*

Alternative 1:

Catch the ferry to Keswick landing stage from High Brandlehowe. Walk distance one and three quarter miles.

4. *Pass High Brandlehowe landing stage and continue through woodland. Leave the woods by a kissing gate in a stone wall, and continue to Low Brandlehowe landing stage .*

Alternative 2:

Catch the ferry to Keswick landing stage from Low Brandlehowe. Walk distance two and half miles.

5. *On arriving at Hawse End Bay, follow the wire fence 125 yds inland, turn right at a "T" junction with a stone track crossing path through a wooden gate into open woodland. Follow the stone track to Hawse End. Cross the metal boundary fences by a wooden stile by the lake shore close to Hawse End landing stage.*

Alternative 3:

Catch the ferry to Keswick landing stage from Hawse End. Walk distance three and one quarter miles.

6. *From the headland, go back into the woodland and continue around the lake shore through a kissing gate. Follow the good path through the woods, through a hole in the fence, to meet the drive leading to Hawse End Outward Bound Centre. Immediately after the junction of another tarmac drive, take the public footpath to the right through a kissing gate towards Portinscale and Keswick.*

7. *The path passes through wire fences, woodland, and streams. Go through a wooden gate in a wire fence and across a meadow. On the far side of the meadow, go through another kissing gate back into woodland. The path passes close to Lingholm Gardens (well worth a side-tracked visit in the Spring time). Go through a wooden gate across the drive to Lingholm, then follow the path on the other side of the drive beside a stone wall. Follow the curving stone track, ignoring turnings to either left or right. Cross the drive to the cottage and continue to Nichol End Marine.*

Alternative 4:

Catch the ferry to Keswick landing stage from Nichol End. Walk distance four and half miles.

8. *Turn left along the access drive and turn right on meeting the public tarmac road towards the village of Portinscale.*

9. *On reaching the "T" junction by the village store, turn right along the lane by the Derwent Water hotel. Cross the suspension footbridge over the river. On meeting the road, ignore the first turning on the right. Take the second turning,off the road, along the path, across the water meadows back to Keswick. Return through the town centre down to the landing stage.*

Causey Pike and Scar Crag Ridge

Height: 2,205 feet. 672 metres. Grading: Strenuous

Outline

Stonycroft – Rowling End – Causey Pike – Scar Crags – Sail Pass – Stonycroft Gill – Stonycroft

Summary

A ridge walk, tackling steep ascents and involving some scrambling approaching the summit of Causey Pike.

Attractions

This is an airy and exciting excursion along the very beautiful ridge between Causey Pike and Scar Crags, which is reached after an interesting and steep rock scramble to the first peak. Our children regard this ridge as being "Man Mountain", because it's profile viewed from Mirehouse resembles a recumbent giant. However, this point of view may require a modicum of imagination, so those readers who can engage in such thoughts may be amused at the thought of climbing over the neck, chin and face of the giant, followed by a return to the valley down his shoulder and arm. Other readers may possibly not share these indulgences, but will then need to find other encouragements to help tired children's limbs along the steeper sections.

In view of the strenuous and, in parts, scrambly nature of this walk, it is enthusiastically recommended for older children who have some experience of steep places. But others may find it to be less enjoyable.

The children will think that they have climbed the Matterhorn and some parents may suffer similar delusions. The highest altitude of the walk is Scar Crags at 2,205 feet, but it may seem to be a lot higher to tired limbs.

This walk is a classic and is said to have been a favourite family excursion for Robert Southey and his children.

Refreshments

The Coledale Inn is a very welcoming walkers' pub, serving substantial nourishment, overlooking Braithwaite village.

Route 8

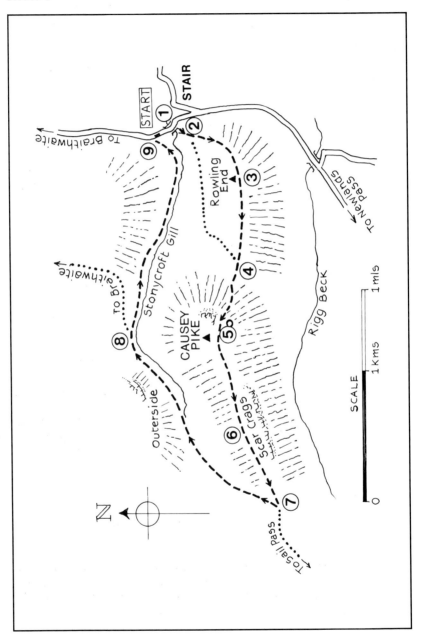

Route 8

Causey Pike and Scar Crag Ridge   5¼ miles

Start
Stonycroft Bridge, by Stair (O.S. grid ref.: NY 232212); lying on the Braithwaite to Newlands road.

Route
1. *Follow the footpath which goes south from the bridge, directly up the steep fellside to Stony croft Gill.*

2. *After walking for about one quarter of a mile, and climbing 200 feet (approximately 60 metres), look out for a fainter track to your left, and follow it as it steeply zigzags over rock outcrops to the top of Rowling End.*

   It is sensible to judge if your family encounters too much difficulty over these steep contours, before trying to cope with the crags which must be surmounted just below the summit of the main ridge.

Alternative Route
It is possible to continue (from point 2 above) along the main path, which climbs more gradually to meet the ridge at Sleet Hawse (point 4 below). Although easier, this alternative misses the enjoyment of walking a superb length of ridge and avoids the steeper scrambly sections over the lower rock outcrops.

3. *Turn West to stride along the gentle top of the Rowling End Ridge.*

4. *Rejoin the Alternative Route at Sleet Hause and commence the climb up the final portion of Causey Pike.*

   Scramble up the crags guarding the summit ridge of Causey Pike. The route should not be too difficult for older children, but parents must keep an eye on them; and, as elsewhere in the fells, should not let them run on to tackle these rocks without close supervision.

5. *Follow the summit ridge, from Causey Pike to Scar Crags.*

6. *Continue along the ridge, down from the summit of Scar Crags, for approximately one quarter of a mile, to meet Sail Pass.*

7. *Turn sharp right and follow the descending track across the scree above Ling Comb. This track continues in a North Easterly direction to arrive at the flattish area of High Moss. Do not be tempted off this track, onto the fainter path which descends steeply to the left, into the deep valley of Coledale.*

41

8. *Continue down the track below the lower South Eastern slopes of Outerside, and fork right to follow the rough track which follows the Northern bank of Stonycroft Gill.*

9. *Follow this track back down to Stonycroft Bridge.*

Along the Causey Pike − Scar Crag Ridge

Outerside and Barrow

Height − 1,863 feet. 568 metres. Grading: Moderate

Outline

Braithwaite − Outerside − Barrow − Braithwaite

Summary

A lovely striding route over grassy tops; quite steep in places.

Attractions

This is a journey into less frequently visited gentle fells within the arms of the higher "Coledale Horseshoe". It is an invigorating, but not excessively taxing, walk with beautiful views to Skiddaw and the lower reaches of Borrowdale

These fells are part of the group named by Coleridge as the "camp of giants' tents". You need to view them from the other side of Keswick to appreciate the aptness of this description.

Words of Caution

Short lengths of this walk are not very distinct, and some of the junctions between paths may possibly be missed; so we do not recommend taking a family in misty conditions. On a clear day, the route is plainly obvious to see.

Refreshments

The Coledale Inn at the western edge of Braithwaite, and overlooking the village, offers substantial nourishment, and families are welcome.

Route 9

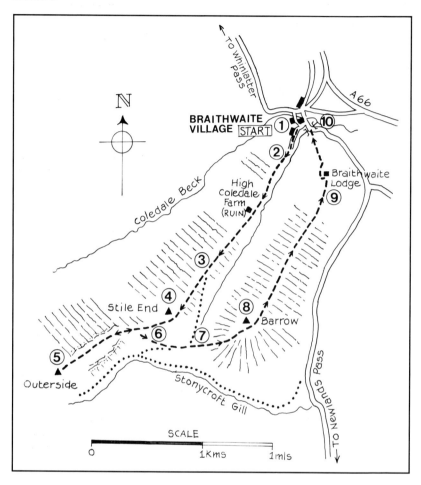

Route 9

Outerside and Barrow

5½ miles
(with 4¾ mile alternative)

Start

This walk commences at the western end of the village of Braithwaite; below the Coledale Inn, off the B5292, just before it starts it's ascent of Whinlatter Pass (O.S. Grid Reference NY 229235)

Route

1. Walk up the tarmaced lane which climbs up to, and to the left (East) of the Coledale Inn. Follow this lane, which continues to rise quite steeply past houses and bungalows on your right and a deep ravine on your left.

2. On reaching the end of the tarmaced lane, climb a stile next to a field gate and walk up the old farm track, passing the sad ruins of High Coledale farm to your right, and continue along the obvious track uphill.

3. Approximately ¼ mile beyond High Coledale farm, branch to the right, up a grassy and less distinct path, which aims directly for the top of Stile End. Ignore the other grassy path which branches further right to contour below the fell.

4. From the summit of Stile End, stroll, in a South-Westerly direction, across the depression of Low Moss, and climb the opposite fell.

5. This is the summit of Outerside, and at 1,863 feet (568 metres), the highest point of the walk. Retrace your steps for approximately ¼ mile back down to Low Moss.

6. Veer to the right (South-East) to meet the main path (between Braithwaite and Sail Pass). Keep Stile End to your left, and ignore the wide track going steeply downhill alongside the gill to your right. There are so many choices of route in this particularly small area, that you will need to be very careful in taking the correct path.

7. Follow the Braithwaite path, for approximately 100 yards, to Barrow Door (a small pass between Stile End and Barrow) then branch right to climb the ridge of Barrow. 1,494 feet (455 metres).

Less strenuous alternative overleaf

Alternative Route

From Barrow Door (point 7 above), continue in a North Easterly direction down the main path to Braithwaite village, thus missing both the delights and extra exertion of climbing over Barrow Fell.

8. *From the summit of Barrow, descend, in a North-Easterly direction down the ridge, along a broad grassy track.*

9. *Go through a wooden gate in a stone wall into an enclosed field, and continue down the signposted route to Braithwaite Lodge farm. Cross the stile and follow the signposted bridleway through the left part of the farmyard and out onto the broad driveway. Follow the driveway down to the public road.*

10. *Turn left upon meeting the public road, and return to Braithwaite village.*

The Keswick boat landings

Cockshot Wood

Grading: easy

Outline

Keswick (Lakeside car-park) − through and around Cockshot Wood −
Keswick (Lakeside car-park)

Summary

An undemanding ramble through woods and meadows and along the lake shore.

Attractions

This is an excellent little walk for young children, which quickly takes you away from
the noise and bustle of Keswick and the boat landings, into peaceful meadows and
woodland. We were lucky to see both deer and red squirrels when we last walked this
route. There is the added attraction that an alternative route is available enabling you
to take the pushchair along the meadow path and to return by the lakeside edge. (This
is our only pushchair walk).

Great fun can be obtained on this alternative short walk by the use of numerous
fallen logs which can be used in fantasy games. Have you ever used a log to play
shipwrecks or "Swallows and Amazons" besides the lakeshore?

Refreshments

The Lakeside Tea Gardens near to the Keswick boat landings.

Route 10

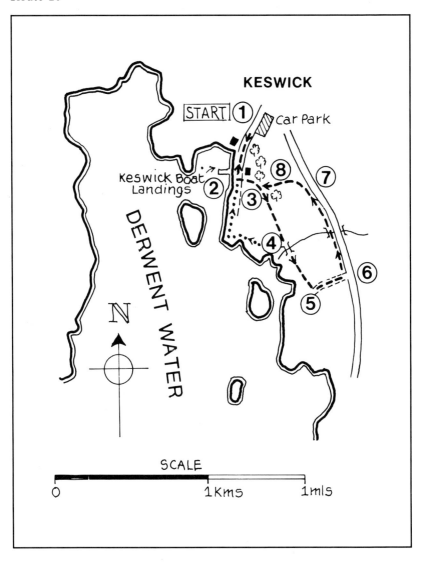

Route 10

Cockshot Wood   2¾ miles

Start

Begin this walk at the Lakeside car park, between the town of Keswick and Derwentwater (O.S. Grid reference NY 265229)

Route

1. *Walk south from the car park, following the tarmac road towards the lake. Continue on the main path past the boat landings.*

2. *Towards the end of the boat landings, and immediately after passing the public conveniences, turn left up a footpath signposted to Cockshot Wood.*
   Upon entering the wood, fork left along the path, following the perimeter of the wood.

3. *Follow this woodland path until you meet a gate, which you pass through and walk across the meadow facing you, taking advantage of the stepping stones over the wetter portions.*

4. *Upon meeting the lakeside footpath, turn left, cross a footbridge over a small stream, and pass through a gate into more woodland. Follow this footpath, through the woodland and over a substantial footbridge after crossing another stream.*

Alternative Route:

On meeting the lake shore (point 4 above), turn right and follow the main path alongside the lake. This path curves round the shore and enters the woodland through a gate to Friar's Cragg – a famous beauty spot. Return along the lakeshore to the car-park, taking in the wonderful views, across the lake, of the surrounding hills and the possibility of a trip on one of the boats.

5. *Leave this wood through another gate and turn left to walk along a farm drive.*

6. *After passing a cattle-grid meet the Borrowdale Road.*

7. *Turn left along the track which is separated alternately by stone walling and hedging from the road. There are some gaps in this barrier, and the road can be busy, so do not let young children run on too far ahead.*

8. *After following this footpath for approximately half a mile, turn left to follow the footpath signposted "To the Lake".*
   Re-enter woodland at a crossroads of footpaths and walk straight on to rise up and over the hill in front of you. Drop down the other side of the hill to rejoin the original path entering the wood from the west side (Point 2 above).

49

Sale Fell

Sale Fell

Height 1,170 feet. 357 metres. Grading: Easy

Outline

Wythop Church – path towards Kelswick – summit of Sale Fell –
Wythop Church

Summary

A gentle grassy ridge walk

Attractions

An attractive and easy "mini-peak" offering a very safe and satisfying first fell for
younger children, giving extensive views around the north western fringe of the Lake
District, over Bassenthwaite and on towards Derwent Water. The prospect of Skiddaw
is very dominant to the east, whilst there is considerable interest within the expansive
vistas to the north and west across the coastal plains, the Solway Firth and onto the
distant hills of Galloway. These comprise the old border-lands of England, being the
North-West frontier of Elizabethan times.

Children of all ages should be fascinated by the nearby working water mill
powering its operating wood working machinery.

Refreshments

There is a cafe within Wythop Mill which serves home baking.

Route 11

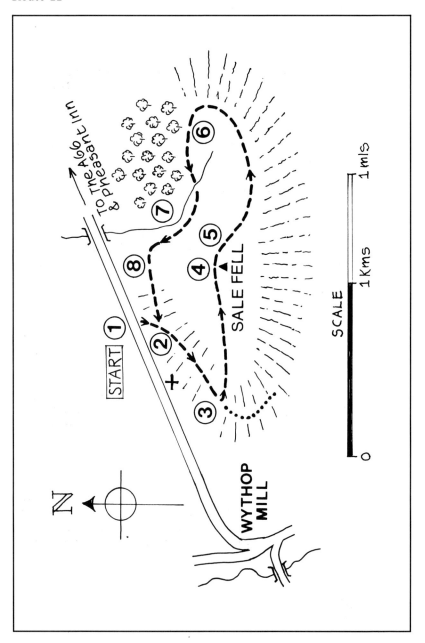

52

Route 11

Sale Fell   2 miles

Start

This walk commences where the path to Kelswick leaves the lane, approximately one hundred yards to the east of the church (O.S. Grid reference NY 193303), and is approached off the A66 following the signpost to Wythop Mill.

Route

1. *Pass through a kissing gate to follow the track slanting up the fellside and signposted to Kelswick.*

2. *Pass through a second kissing gate and turn right along the track that contours around the fell.*

3. *After approximately a further half of a mile this track contours to the left into the entrance of Wythop valley. When the track starts to descend, strike out to your left following the gently climbing broad ridge between the gorse and the bracken.*

4. *The summit of the fell is reached after approximately a further half of a mile up this path*

5. *To descend, follow the path to the south east, around the head of the coombe, with the steeper slope to your left, passing through two wide gaps in the stone walls crossing your route.*

6. *Turn left when you reach the stone wall bounding the conifer plantation ahead of you, and follow the narrow track, through the bracken down into the valley. The path crosses the stream and passes through a gap in a stone wall, then continues downwards, roughly parallel to the beck.*

7. *The path curves to the left along a shelf in the steep fellside.*

8. *When the church comes back into view, take the narrow path contouring around the fell to your left. Do not follow the more direct descents down the fell. The path broadens out to a grassy track again and joins the route of ascent at point 2. Turn acutely right, and descend, through the kissing gate, to regain the lane at the foot of the fell.*

The summit of Sale Fell

Latrigg

Height 1,203 feet. 367 metres. Grading: Moderate

Outline

Spoony Green Lane (Keswick) – Latrigg – Spoony Green Lane (Keswick)

Summary

A gentle "Mini Peak" nestling under Skiddaw. Yet another mountain that gives the younger members of the party the opportunity to feel they have achieved a summit, without feeling totally exhausted at the end of the day.

Attractions

There are lovely woodland tracks to follow, which gradually wind their way up the mountainside. After a final pull to the top, the view is expansive across Derwentwater and the mountain terrain, which Coleridge described as "A camp of giants' tents". How many "tents" can your children count?

It is quite often possible to watch people hang-gliding off the summit of Latrigg.

Refreshments

Either your own picnic, or refreshments are obtainable in Keswick.

Route 12

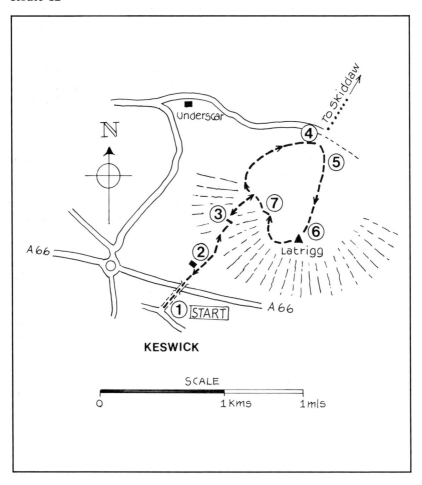

Route 12

Latrigg

3¼ miles

Start

This walk is commenced at the lower end of Spoony Green Lane on the northern edge of Keswick (O.S. Grid Reference NY 267242), which can be reached by following the old signpost towards the sadly defunct "Railway Station" from the A591.

Route

1. *Walk up the Spoony Green Lane bridleway, and follow the stone lane over the bridge above the by-pass.*

2. *Continue past the cottage on your left, and through a kissing gate into the woods. Follow the broad forest track along the edge of the forest. (Ignore turnings or gateways to left or right into the forest).*

3. *After a further half a mile, follow the first set of zig zags, (ignoring the newer forest track to the right). Cross the beck and pass through a kissing gate. The path follows through gorse and bracken and then rejoins the edge of the forest.*

4. *Continue past a carved stone post up the final zig zags to the coll between Latrigg and Skiddaw (about one and a half miles from the start) alongside the end of the metalled road*

Alternative Easy Option Route

A car can be driven up to this point (O.S. grid reference 282253), by following the steep narrow metalled Gale Road from Underscar (O.S. grid reference 267257). This provides an easier and shorter route.

5. *Turn right before kissing gate, follow the fence line for approximately fifty yards and then turn South to climb up the grassy slope to the skyline (Ignore the grass path to the right).*

6. *Stroll over the turf to the top and enjoy the panoramic views.*

7. *Drop down off the summit, head to the bench and the viewpoint. Retrace your steps and join the path on your left heading North. This path gently descends and zig zags down to meet your route of ascent (note point 4). Turn left and follow the forest path along the original route of ascent to Spoony Lane.*

The bridleway up towards the church

High Rigg

Height 1,163 feet. 354 metres. Grading: Moderate

Outline

Legburthwaite car park − St.John's church − High Rigg summit − Legburthwaite car park.

Summary

A valley walk, with the return over a knobbly ridge.

Attractions

The walk initially follows the pastoral valley of St.John's In The Vale, through mixed woodland and open fellside under steep crags; then climbs up and over the "rollercoaster" ridge of High Rigg. Our children have enjoyed following the "Giants' Footsteps" to the top of each little summit, followed by the brief cruise down the short slope then repeating the sequence over the next rise.

The views are beautiful across Thirlmere, and northwards to the south face of Blencathra, which looks positively Himalayan when draped with snow.

The attractive little fell top church of St.John's may be visited on route.

Refreshments

The nearest hostelry is The King's Arms, which is approximately a mile south down the A591 at Thirlspot.

Route 13

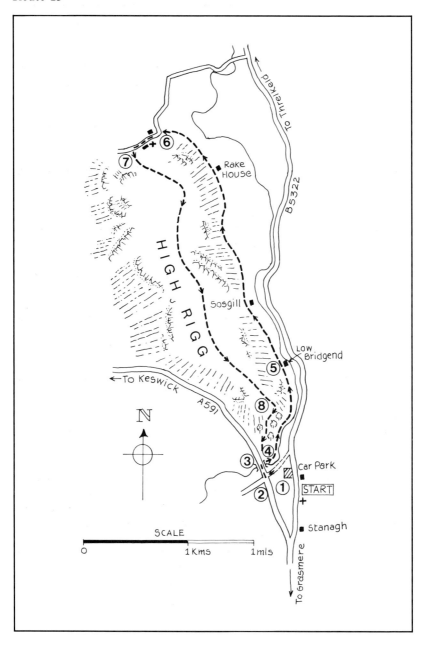

Route 13

High Rigg   4½ miles

Start
Car Park situated at Legburthwaite, and approached by the B5322 approximately one half of a mile off the junction with the A591 (O.S. Grid reference NY 317196)

Route

1. *Leave the car park by its northern exit through a wooden gate in the stone wall, and turn left along the gated tarmaced lane.*

2. *On meeting the main road (A591), turn right and walk along the grass verge to cross the river bridge.*

3. *After following this road, for approximately 50 yards, turn right to cross the timber ladder stile across the high stone wall, and enter the woodland beyond. Take the stony upper path and ignore the grassy lower path.*

4. *Follow the path, signposted to "The Church". Ignore the path branching steeply up the fell to your left. This will be your return route.*

5. *The path contours around the eastern base of the steep fellside, to the uphill side of the intake wall. Pass above Low Bridgend Farm, and continue along the contouring path. Ignore the downhill turn to the North of the farm.*

6. *The path slants up the fellside to meet the narrow tarmaced lane towards the top of the pass across the ridge. Turn left, uphill along this lane.*

Escape Route
It is possible to take a car to the top of the pass, at the church, by driving up the lane which climbs up the eastern flank of the fell out of St. John's vale.

7. *Pass the church, and climb to the left up the grass fell. Go through the wooden gate in the stone wall and follow the path which meanders, in a generally southerly direction, along the hummocky and broad ridge. There are many variations in the paths crisscrossing over the numerous tops and small crags along this fell.*

8. *Descend along the path down the south extremity of the ridge to re-join the route of ascent (point 4 above) and return to the car park.*

IN Memory OF
JOHN PEEL OF
RUTHWAITE, who died
Nov.13th 1854, aged 78 Years.
Also MARY, his wife who
died Aug 9th 1859 aged 82
Also JONATHAN their Son
who died Jan 21st 1806.
aged 2 Years.
Also PETER their Son, who
died Nov 15th 1840.
aged 27 Years.
Also MARY DAVIDSON their
DAUGHTER who died Nov 30
1863, aged 48 Years.
Also JOHN their Son who died
Nov 22nd 1887 aged 50 Years

John Peel's grave

Caldbeck — "The Howk"

Grading: Easy

Outline

Caldbeck — "The Howk" — Todcroft — Upton — Priest Mill — Caldbeck

Summary

A delightful and varied walk, through woodland, river gorge and open fields, passing many points of interest within its short span.

Attractions

This walk, which passes through and around Caldbeck, reveals some of the history of this pretty limestone village. Children will enjoy feeding the marauding ducks on the village pond, and will be unable to resist playing dramatic "pooh sticks" from the bridge over the waterfall. This bridge used to be a natural rock span, but it was dynamited in 1817 by the local farmer who was unimpressed by its use as a right of way. Modern ramblers are not made so unwelcome.

The "Howk" is a deep and impressive limestone gorge (which is a unique feature for this area) where a bobbin mill remains as only a beautiful ruin. The wheel, long since gone, was argued to be the largest in the country when it was installed in 1857, having a diameter of 42 feet and a width of 3 feet.

Many will be drawn towards St.Kentigern's church, which dates from the mid 12th century, and even incorporates fragments from the 8th century. John Peels' grave (the famous huntsman) can also be found there. The craft shops at Priests Mill should entertain all ages. The working water wheel is of great interest.

Refreshments

Refreshments: There are two restaurants within the village of Caldbeck.

Route 14

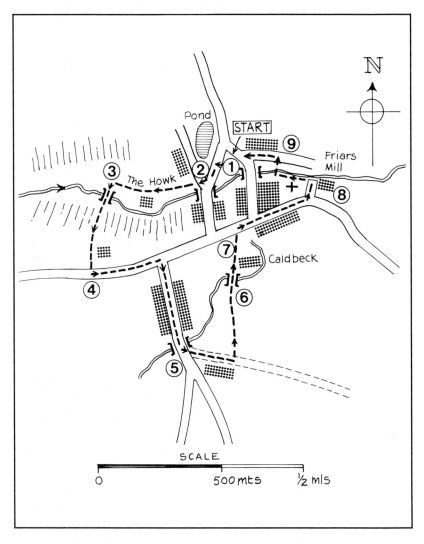

Route 14

Caldbeck – "The Howk" 1¾ miles

Start

The walk starts from the car park off the B5299 (O.S. Grid reference NY 323399) on the outskirts of the village.

Route

1. *Walk upstream past the entrance to a house called "Deer Park", up the hill, to the village pond, and turn left along the lane.*

2. *At a "T" junction, walk to the left of a stone barn, and follow the footpath sign to "The Howk". Pass through the yard and the two consecutive kissing gates. Continue past the old mill, and walk into the limestone gorge and up the steep steps to a wonderful view of the waterfall.*

3. *Turn left to drop down the path, to cross over the footbridge above the waterfall. Climb up the path on the opposite side and go through the kissing gate into a large open field. Aim for the coppice of Scots Pines to the right of the grey stone farmhouse across the other side of the field. The kissing gate is just to the right of the coppice.*

4. *Turn left down the lane. Be careful of the traffic. Take the first right junction, after about a hundred yards, and immediately before the village school.*

5. *Directly after the hump back bridge, over the stream, fork left up the tractor track, in front of a row of cottages. Immediately after the cottages turn left over a steep stone stile into a large field. Veer left, following the hedge and fence boundary, so that you will not miss the stile towards the lower end of the field. The stile is marked with a yellow arrow.*
   Look out for the two distinctive, tall, white windmills turning in the distance to your right.

6. *Drop steeply down to the footbridge by the old mill pond and sluice gate. (Caution, this section is often slippery when wet). Follow the path to the left of a private garden, ignore a wooden stile to your left, and continue round the outside of the garden boundary and along the drive, to its opening into a minor lane.*

7. *Cross the lane and climb up the steep, and very narrow steps within the facing stone wall. Be watchful of traffic at the top of the steps. Wider members of the party may avoid these difficulties by turning right before the steps and rejoining the route within about 50 yards.*

   Turn right at the top of the steps and follow the road into centre of village, past the public toilets and clog makers. Continue past the pub, petrol station, and rectory and St.Kentigurns church. You may wish to see the distinctive grave of John Peel (made famous by a border ballad) to the left of the church door.

8. *Turn left, down stone track, signposted to "Priest Mill" where there is an interesting collection of various craft shops, a restaurant (which has home cooking). The restored mill, has a working wheel and a small museum of milling. The children will also enjoy the hens pecking around the yard.*

9. *Take the path, upstream, between the churchyard wall and the river, and pass over the stone packhorse bridge. Note St.Kentigern's Well below the bridge. Follow the lane, upstream, on the other side of the river and carefully cross the road to return to the car park.*

Sailing in Ullswater

66

Ullswater

Grading: Moderate

Outline

Howtown − Sandwick − Patterdale − Glenridding −
(return on Steamer to Howtown).

Distance can be shortened by 1½ miles, by making an alternative start at Sandwick bay. Note: steamer does not stop there. A car will have to be left there to drive back to meet the rest of the party at Howtown.

Summary

A lakeside walk with return by lake steamer.

Attractions

A good undulating path above the lake shore with panoramic views of the lake, and the length of the Helvellyn range behind. There are, almost invariably, many yachts adding variety to the scene and a speed limit prevents the intrusive noise of outboard engines. The steamers are ''Raven'' and ''Lady of the Lake''.

Children will enjoy the variety of woodland and rocky paths, and watching the boats and steamers with the possibility of being transported back to the start of the route by steamer. Do check the times of the steamer before starting the walk. (Minimum walk time four hours with young children). It's a long way back if you miss the last boat − we know!

Refreshments

Children's portions served at the Ratchers Tavern next to the Glenridding Hotel. On the lake steamers: basic refreshments.

Ensure that plenty of fluid is carried on this walk on a hot day!

Route 15

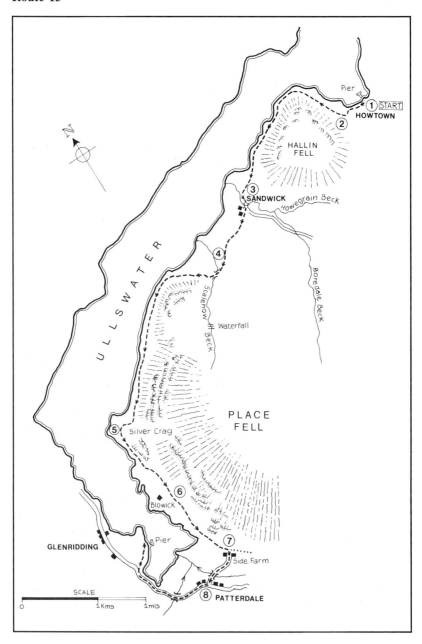

Route 15

Ullswater   6¾ miles

Start

Lake Ullswater Howtown landing stage. Grid reference: NY 443198. Approached by minor roads off the B5320 from Pooley Bridge.

Route

1. *Start the walk at the Howtown landing stage. Cross the wooden footbridge over the beck, and follow the lake shore around Howtown Wyke. After two kissing gates, turn right along a farm track. Turn left through another kissing gate, and follow the signs to Patterdale and Sandwick.*

2. *Follow the path around the edge of the field, climb the steps and pass through another gate and immediately turn right along a stony path contouring round fells above Waternook House.*

3. *At another kissing gate enter deciduous woodland*
   Leaving the woodland, the path follows through fields away from the lake. After about one and a half miles cross the farm bridge over Howe Grain beck, go through the farm gate, turn left up the tarmac lane and take the bridleway around the back of the farmhouses.

4. *Continue along the path and follow the fellside above the lake and through woodlands. Approximately half a mile outside Sandwick, the path crosses Scalehow Beck by a footbridge. A large waterfall can be glimpsed upstream.*

5. *Ignore the farm gate on the right, and continue along the path above the stone walls, now passing beneath the steep ramparts of Place Fell. At 'approximately four miles, you will walk around the headland at Silver Crag and Glenridding pier will come into view. (You will go past Glenridding, around the Southern end of the lake to the pier).*

6. *Opposite Glenridding, the path is enclosed by stone walls and woodland. Continue along a stone track back into open fellside. Ignore any openings or stiles to left or right. Past Blowick house. Continue past, (but do not enter) the campsite. Watch for campsite traffic along this track.*

7. *Follow the stone motor traffic road, ignoring any turnings until you reach Side Farm. Turn right between farm buildings, follow the track across the flat valley floor and over the farm bridge to meet the main road at Patterdale Village Hall.*

69

8. *Turn right, and follow the main road past the church and sports ground, passing over the river and into Glenridding. Follow alternative footpath where available, as it will take you away from the road through woodland. After three-quarter of a mile of road, the path to the Pier strikes off across the fields to the right.*

Enjoy a pleasant saunter along the pier as you await the arrival of your chosen steamer which will return you in a leisurely manner to Howtown.

Ice on Angle Tarn

Angle-Tarn Pikes

Height 1,857 feet (566 metres). Grading: Moderate

Outline

Boardale Head − Boardale Hause − Angle-Tarn Pikes −
Boardale Hause − Boardale Head

Summary

A reasonably graded walk, mainly along clearly defined paths, to a pair of rugged
"mini peaks" overlooking the Patterdale and Glenridding valley.

Attractions

This is a secluded area, with the only road access being along the narrow lane,
following the south-eastern shore of Ullswater and over the very steep Howtown
zigzags. Our opinion is that this is Lakeland at its best.

    This expedition commences in the depths of a remote valley, then climbs to a broad
and interesting ridge giving expansive and spectacular views across the Helvellyn and
High Street mountain ranges.

    There are many pathways through this delightful area, but most are thin and
intermittent, and easily missed by an inexperienced party. This walk cheats a little,
because of the impracticality of forming a circular route on obvious paths and a
substantial section is repeated in both directions. This is no hardship, because it is
exceptionally beautiful and is to be savoured, whichever way you walk.

    The walk passes through what was, until recently, the Lord's hunting ground, and
is close to a deer sanctuary. Walk quietly, if you can, and you may be lucky enough
to see the deer.

Refreshments

Drinks and ice creams are served in the cottage garden at Boardale Head Farm, but
only during peak holiday times.

Route 16

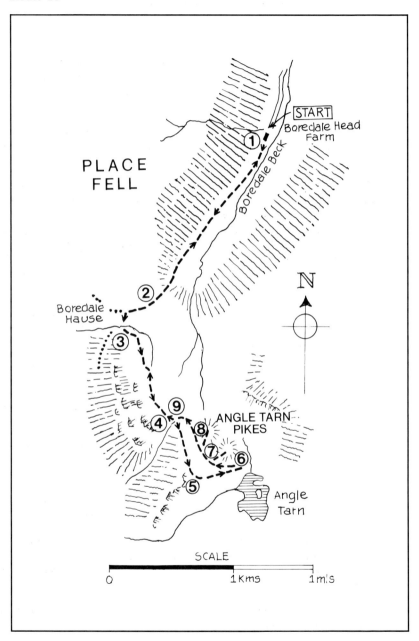

Route 16

Angle-Tarn Pikes   6 miles

Start

Commence your walk from Boardale Head Farm (O.S. Grid reference NY419171). Some attentive map reading is required to drive the narrow lanes, twisting through the dales, from Pooley Bridge to the start of this walk.

Route

1. *Take the bridle path, signposted to Patterdale, through the farmyard. Follow the grassy track which climbs evenly towards the dale head. There is a short, slightly rougher section in the final stretch before the pass.*

2. *The path clambers roughly, out of the head of the valley of Boardale (past the inspection and valve chambers of the water pipeline, which amazingly tunnels through Place Fell from Ullswater).*
   On reaching the pass of Boardale Hause, the grassy path descends gently, between the bracken, in a westerly direction; and meets the obvious path between Patterdale and the distant High Street range. (If you have descended so that Glenridding and Patterdale come into view like toy villages below your feet, then – sorry, but you have walked slightly too far)

3. *Turn left at the prominent cairn, and follow this path, across the stream by the small waterfall, and climb up the fellside. The path climbs through a small ravine, up the stream bed, then curves to the left as it rises over the open fellside.*

4. *Follow the right hand fork in the path, around the head of the small gully, as it contours above the very steep fellside.*

5. *The path rises gently to a rocky shoulder and curves to the left. The view of Angle Tarn unfolds before you.*

6. *Follow the path until you are above the tarn, then turn sharp left, up the slightly thinner track, which climbs higher up the western shoulder to the southern pike.*

7. *On reaching a small cairn, turn right to climb approximately one hundred yards, up an indistinct path, to the southern pike. Retrace your steps, to avoid broken crags and steep ground. Rejoin the main path, and turn right (North-West).*

8. *When the northern pike comes into view, branch right to follow a faint path up a grassy shoulder to the higher summit (1,857 feet, 613 metres). Retrace your steps again, to avoid broken crags and steep ground. Rejoin the main path, and turn right.*

9. *Rejoin route of ascent at point "7" above and return via Boardale Hause and Boardale to the start of the walk.*

73

Looking down to Brothers Water

Useful Information

Explanation of gradings.

Valley walks are graded according to length in preference to steepness or difficulty underfoot.

Fell walks are graded as follows:

Easy: walks of two miles or less, with gentle ascent and not difficult underfoot.

Moderate: walks up to six miles in length involving continous, longer ascents.

Strenous: Rougher walks reccomended for teenagers.

Grading in order of difficulty.

Valley walks   *Distance in miles*

Easier Walks
Route 14	Caldbeck "The Howk"	1.75
Route 6	Johnny's Wood	2.00
Route 10	Cockshot Wood	2.75
Route 4	Buttermere	4.75
Route 7	Derwentwater	6.75

Moderate Walks
Route 15	Ullswater	6.75
Route 1	Ennerdale	7.00

Fell Walks

Easier Walks
Route 11	Sale Fell	2.00

Moderate Walks
Route 12	Latrigg	3.25
Route 3	Rannerdale Knotts	4.00
Route 13	High Rigg	4.50
Route 9	Outerside and Barrow	5.50
Route 16	Angle Tarn Pikes	6.00

Strenuous walks
Route 8	Causey Pike	5.25
Route 2	Mellbreak	5.50
Route 5	Styhead & Sprinkling Tarns	8.00

Wet Weather Alternatives

Beatrix Potter Gallery: Hawksehead (015394) 46601. National Trust. (Open April to early November). A collection of original drawings for her books can be seen here.

Hill Top: Sawrey. (015394) 36269. National Trust. (Open April to early November). The home of Beatrix Potter, the author of Jemima Puddle Duck and Peter Rabbit etc.

World of Beatrix Potter exhibition: Bowness (015394) 45565. (Open daily, last entrance 3.30p.m.) A magical experience for both the old and young. We all enjoyed it!

Brockhole National Park Visitors centre: Windermere (015394) 46601. (Open April to early November). An appreciation of the topography and history of the Lake District.

Cumberland Pencil Museum: Keswick (017686) 73626. (Open daily, closed Christmas & New Year). An exhibition of Borrowdale graphite usage in pencil making.

Cumberland Toy and Model Museum: Cockermouth (01900) 827606. (Open February to November).

Stott Park Bobbin Mill: Newby Bridge (015394) 31087. Victorian steam engine. Belt- driven, bobbin turning mill. Very realistic!

Whythop Mill: Embleton (017687) 76394. (Open March to October, closed Mondays) Woodworking museum. Working water wheel, display of woodworking tools and blacksmiths equipment.

Museum of Lakeland Life and Industry: Kendal (01539) 722464. (Open daily, reduced hours in Winter7 A display of daily life and times.

Tullie house: Carlisle (01228) 34781. (Open daily) A history of the borders — Romans to modern day. Well worth visiting!

Windermere Steam Boat Museum: Windermere (015394) 45565. (Easter to October). A collection of full size steam, motor and sailing boats.

Ravenglass and Eskdale Railway: Ravenglass (01229) 717171. (Open daily, reduced service Winter). Seven miles from the coast to the hills on small steam trains.

Gardens

Mire house: Keswick (017687) 72287 or 74317 (Open March to October). Excellent adventure playground! Forest and Lakeside walks.

Levens Hall: Sedgwick (015395) 60321. (Open April to September, Sunday-Thursday). Steam collection. Excellent topiary.

Sizergh Castle: Kendal (015395) 60070. (Open April to October). National Trust. Contains the National Trusts largest rock garden.

Garden Centre

Hayes: Ambleside (015394) 33434. (Open daily except Xmas/New Year). Play area, exotic fish and plants, outdoor gardens, greenhouses and coffee shop. An absolute must for the avid or vaguely interested gardener!

Woodland and Forest Trails

Grizedale Forest Park: near Hawkeshead (01229) 860373. (Open daily), sculpture trail map available from local pub. Several graded and waymarked walks. Exciting carved scupltures found throughout the forest.

Whinlatter Visitor Centre: Whinlatter Pass — Keswick (017687) 78469. (Open daily). Forestry commission. Permanent orienteering courses, forest and geology trails, exhibition and adventure playground.

Country Parks

Lowther Leisure Park: near Penrith (019312) 523. (Open Easter, Spring bank holiday to early September). Excellent adventure playground and circus for the younger members of the family.
Fell Foot Park: Newby Bridge (015395) 71273. (Open all year). An 18 acre country park. Bathing area, adventure playground, boating, picnic area and cafe.

Farm Experiences

Lakeland Bird of Prey Centre: Lowther, near Penrith (01931) 712746. (Open daily March to October). Flying displays thrice daily. Aviary walks. One day courses, tea shop.
Trotters and Friends: Keswick (017687) 76239. (Open March to October). An opportunity to feed and stroke the animals. Farming calendar followed with events for children; help milk the cows.
Four Seasons Farm Experience: Calthwaite near Penrith (016974) 73309/73753. An excellent display of farm birds, goats, and deer. The opportunity to make butter and bread. Childrens playground.

Swimming pools

Keswick Leisure Pool: (017687) 72760
Penrith: (01768) 63450
Appleby-in-Westmorland: Open air (summer only) (017683) 51212
Troutbeck: near Windermere (015394) 43243

Public Transport Operators

Applicable to the Walks

British Rail:
   Barrow-in-Furness (01229) 820805
   Carlisle (01228) 44711
Cumberland Motor Services: Whitehaven (01946) 63222
National Travel: (contact Cumberland or Ribble Motor services)
Ribble Motor Services: Lancaster (01524) 64228
Mountain Goat Bus-Company: Windermere (015394) 45161
Keswick Launch Company: Keswick (017687) 72263
Ullswater Navigation & Transit Co.:
   Kendal (01539) 721626
   Glenridding (017684) 82229
Windermere Vehicle Ferry: Kendal (01539) 20251
Ravenglass & Eskdale Railway Co.: Ravenglass (01229) 717171

National Park Information Centres

24 Hour Weather Forecast: (017687) 75757
Bowness Bay: (015394) 42895
Coniston: (015394) 41533
Grasmere: (015394) 35245
Glenridding: (017684) 82414
Hawkshead: (015394) 36525
Keswick: (017687) 72803
Pooley Bridge: (017684) 86530
Seatoller: (017687) 77294
Waterhead: 015394) 32729

Recipes

GRASMERE GINGERBREAD
Ingredients
1lb plain flour ½lb soft brown sugar
1 teaspoon bicarbonate of soda
½lb butter (or margarine)
2 teaspoons of ground ginger

Method
Rub in all dry ingredients and place in oblong flat tin, previously greased. Cut while hot. Cook in a moderate oven 10-15 minutes.

FELL'S FLAPJACK
Ingredients
4 oz margarine
4oz soft brown sugar
3oz syrup
8oz rolled oats
handful of raisins

Method
Melt margarine, sugar and syrup together in bowl over a pan of boiling water. Add oats and raisins and mix well. Put into greased 8″ square tin and bake at Gas mark 4 for 30 minutes. Leave for 10 minutes before cutting into fingers and allow to cool before taking out of tin.

BORROWDALE TEA BREAD
Ingredients
½lb currants'
1lb self raising flour
½lb sultanas
1 egg
½lb demerara sugar
2 tablespoons thick marmalade

Method
Soak the fruit in tea for several hours. Beat the eggs and add them with the flour to the fruit. Mix well and pour into a 2lb loaf tin. Bake for about 2 hours at 350°F/180°C (gas mark 4). Turn out and cool.

THE FAMILY WALKS SERIES

The publishers welcome suggestions for future titles and will be pleased to consider manuscripts relating to Derbyshire from new and established authors.

Scarthin Books of Cromford, in the Peak District, are also leading new, second-hand and antiquarian booksellers, and are eager to purchase specialised material, both ancient and modern.

Contact Dr. D.J. Mitchell 01629 823272.

. . . and if ever in the PEAK District, do visit:

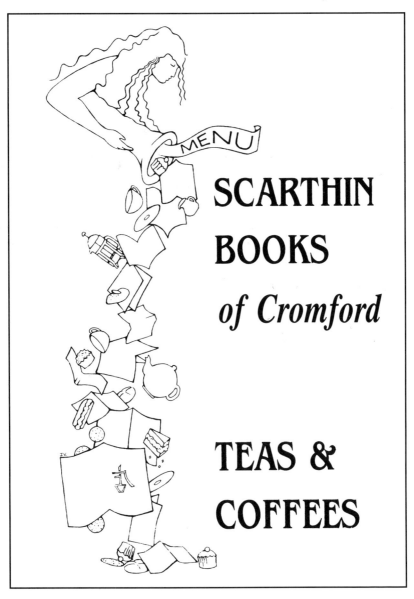

SCARTHIN

BOOKS

of Cromford

TEAS &

COFFEES

A Bookshop for the Majority of Minorities
Open 10 – 6, 12 – 6 Sundays. Tel: 01629 – 823272